D1562803

POWER
SMOOTHIES

52 Recipes for Smoothies
with Superfood Power

Ellen Brown with **Karen Konopelski Hensley**

© 2014 Fair Winds Press
Text © 2008 Fair Winds Press

First published in the USA in 2014 by
Fair Winds Press, a member of
Quayside Publishing Group
100 Cummings Center, Suite 406-L
Beverly, MA 01915-6101
www.fairwindspress.com

Visit www.QuarrySPOON.com and help us celebrate food and culture
one spoonful at a time!

18 17 16 15 14   1 2 3 4 5

ISBN: 978-1-59233-629-6

Cover and book design by Laura H. Couallier, Laura Herrmann Design
Photography by Glenn Scott Photography and www.shutterstock.com

Printed and bound in China

*The information in this book is for educational purposes only. It is not
intended to replace the advice of a physician or medical practitioner. Please
see your health care provider before beginning any new health program.*

THE SMOOTHIE RECIPES

INTRODUCTION

Smoothies fill the niche when you
want a food that tastes decadent
during the day or at the end of a
meal, but you also want it to be
good for you. Smoothies are the
healthful grandchildren of the
malteds and milkshakes of my
youth, and they can be created
from a cornucopia of nutritious
fruits and other beneficial ingredients. For breakfast they are the
perfect "car cuisine" because they
can be sipped while driving. They
are a flavorful treat for children
and adults at any time of day, and
they make wonderful desserts, too.

The smoothies in *Power Smoothies* accomplish much more than
quenching your thirst with thick and frosty drinks. I chose specific
ingredients that contain the nutrients you need to keep your all-
important immune system in optimal condition. The immune
system has a vital role in protecting your body from disease and
fighting infection if it does invade.

SMOOTHIE BASICS

The good news is that these nutrient-packed drinks are incredibly easy to make; if you can push a button, you can make a smoothie. And chances are you already own a blender—the key appliance you need for making smoothies. If not, it is a small investment for the substantial benefits that drinking smoothies can bring to your health.

The blender is your secret to smoothie success because it has the power to create a thick and frosty concoction from a combination of chilled and frozen ingredients on which all smoothies are based. Here you will learn about blenders, the simple logic of smoothie-making, and how to "dress up" the finished drink with super easy and healthful garnishes.

CHOOSING AND USING A BLENDER OR SMOOTHIE MAKERS

In many kitchens, a food processor has taken the place of a blender, and as much as I depend on my food processor, blenders really do a better job at making smoothies. The large blade and the overall shape of a food processor's work bowl do not aerate the smoothie mixture to produce a creamy, thick texture to the same degree as a blender. Additionally, food processors do not crush ice as effectively; therefore, if you plan to use a food processor to make a smoothie, you should first crush the ice into pieces no larger than a lima bean.

Safety First

As with all electrical appliances, the first precaution is to remember that a blender should be grounded and the cord should not be frayed in any way. Always unplug the blender before wiping the base clean, and never submerge the base in water; scrub it on the counter and rinse with a sponge or paper towels.

HOW TO MAKE A LUSCIOUS SMOOTHIE

To make a smoothie you need something solid to thicken the mixture, something liquid to give it a drinkable consistency, and something to bind these two types of ingredients once they have been emulsified.

In general, a smoothie's thickness is determined by the proportion of frozen ingredients to liquid ingredients. The greater number of frozen ingredients, the thicker the smoothie will be. If you like really chilled and really thick smoothies, you should use more frozen ingredients. If you like your drinks only slightly thicker than fruit juice, then make the smoothie from only chilled ingredients (you will still achieve some thickness from the fiber in the fruit).

The higher the water content of a particular fruit, the less texture it will add to the drink. For example, slices of banana will make a smoothie far thicker than cubes of watermelon. Watermelon is more than 90 percent water, so once it is puréed, you have a lot of pink water without much texture. Another quality of fruit that dictates how much texture it will add to the smoothie is the amount of fiber it contains. Pineapple, for instance, has more fiber than peaches, so it will add more body to the drink. The fiber content is listed for each smoothie recipe, so you will be able to judge which fruits offer the most fiber.

Blending Protocol

The first step in making a smoothie is to briefly blend any liquids and other refrigerated ingredients. This initial blending creates a matrix in which it is easier to purée the frozen ingredients. The length of time required for this initial blending is determined by what ingredients are being blended. If the mixture is primarily liquid, or a soft solid like yogurt or silken tofu, then twenty seconds is sufficient. However, if your chilled ingredients include such fibrous foods as strawberries or apples, forty-five seconds is the recommended time. But let your eye be the judge; you want these ingredients to be totally puréed before adding frozen ingredients to the beaker.

Serving Smoothies for Dessert

While smoothies can be served with some simple cookies for a delicious dessert, you can also go one step further and turn your smoothie into your own homemade frozen treat, similar in texture and flavor to ice cream or frozen yogurt. And you don't need an expensive machine to accomplish this task (although it can be done in an ice cream maker if you own one).

In either case, make the smoothie according to the recipe directions. If using an ice cream machine, follow the manufacturer's instructions after preparing the smoothie. If not using an ice cream machine, pour the smoothie mixture into a 9 × 13-inch (23 × 33-cm) pan, and place it in the freezer. When it has partially frozen—the consistency will be similar to that of a snow cone—scrape the mixture into a mixing bowl and beat it well with an electric mixer. Repeat this entire process two more times, then scrape the mixture into a storage container and freeze until solid. Enjoy!

ABOUT THE AUTHORS

Ellen Brown is the founding food editor of *USA Today* and the author of more than thirty cookbooks, most of which focus on a single food or style of cooking. She wrote nine books on topics as varied as smoothies and fondue to fast and fresh meals as part of the popular *The Complete Idiot's Guide* series, and also wrote a five-volume set on regional American grilling. Her titles also include the award-winning *Gourmet Gazelle Cookbook*, and *Scoop*, which features more than 125 different ice creams adapted from the nation's best creameries.

Ellen now writes a weekly column for the *Providence Journal*, and her writing has appeared in more than two dozen publications, including the *Washington Post*, the *Los Angeles Times*, *Bon Appétit*, *Art Culinaire*, *Texas Monthly*, *The Baltimore Sun*, and the *San Francisco Chronicle*.

Honored by *Cook's Illustrated* in the prestigious "Who's Who of Cooking in America," Ellen has been profiled in *The Washington Post*, *The Detroit News*, *Coastal Living*, and *The Miami Herald*.

She lives in Providence, Rhode Island.

Karen Konopelski Hensley, M.S., R.D., is the dietitian at University of Richmond where she provides one-on-one counseling to students, staff, and faculty on issues ranging from weight management, eating disorders, sports nutrition, and healthy eating. Additionally, she works with students with special dietary needs such as celiac disease and works with the dining hall staff to create healthy food options. She has also worked at Virginia Commonwealth University, Princeton University, and the University of Connecticut.

B-BOOSTING
BANANA APRICOT SMOOTHIE

B-BOOSTING
BANANA APRICOT SMOOTHIE

You cannot find a fruit with as much essential vitamin B6—which helps maintain the health of your organs—as bananas. They are also rich in potassium, an important mineral that balances the electrolytes in your body, especially after exercise. A banana's mild flavor and creamy texture makes it a natural to match with perky apricots, a good source of vitamin A and the antioxidant lycopene.

- 1½ cups (355 ml) chilled apricot nectar
- 3 fresh apricots, seeded and diced
- 2 ounces (55 g) dried apricots, diced
- ¼ cup (32 g) whey protein powder
- 2 tablespoons (30 g) bee pollen
- 2 cups (300 g) banana slices, frozen
- 4 dried apricots for garnish (optional)

▨ Combine apricot nectar, fresh apricots, dried apricots, whey protein powder, and bee pollen in a blender or smoothie maker. Blend on high speed for 45 seconds or until mixture is puréed and smooth. Add banana slices, and blend on high speed again until mixture is smooth. Serve immediately, garnished with dried apricots, if desired.

▨ **YIELD:** Four 1-cup (235-ml) servings

CULLING THE COPPER
BANANA SESAME SMOOTHIE

CULLING THE COPPER
BANANA SESAME SMOOTHIE

Copper is the mineral linked most often with relieving the pain of rheumatoid arthritis, a prevalent autoimmune disease, and sesame seeds—the basis for tahini—are among the best sources of this trace mineral. Their flavor is subtle and blends nicely with that of potassium-rich bananas.

1 cup (235 ml) plain soy milk
½ cup (120 ml) silken tofu
½ cup (120 g) tahini
¼ cup (30 g) sesame seeds
¼ cup (85 g) honey
2 tablespoons (30 g) bee pollen
½ teaspoon (2.5 ml) pure vanilla extract
2 cups (300 g) banana slices, frozen
2 tablespoons (15 g) toasted sesame seeds for garnish (optional)

■ Combine soy milk, tofu, tahini, sesame seeds, honey, bee pollen, and vanilla extract in a blender or smoothie maker. Blend on high speed for 20 seconds or until mixture is puréed and smooth. Add banana slices, and blend on high speed again until mixture is smooth. Serve immediately, garnished with sesame seeds, if desired.

■ **YIELD:** Four 1-cup (235-ml) servings

FAB FOR FIBER
RASPBERRY BANANA SMOOTHIE

FAB FOR FIBER
RASPBERRY BANANA SMOOTHIE

Your immune system does not exist in a vacuum; it is one of the systems that your body needs to keep in working order at all times. The dietary fiber in both raspberries and bananas is important to keep your gastrointestinal system working well. The nutrients in these two fruits boost your immune system too.

1 container (8 ounces or 225 g) raspberry low-fat yogurt
½ cup (120 ml) silken tofu
¼ cup (80 g) fruit-only raspberry preserves
1 cup (150 g) sliced banana
¼ cup (32 g) whey protein powder
2 tablespoons (30 g) bee pollen
1½ cups (190 g) raspberries, frozen
½ cup (70 g) vanilla frozen yogurt
12 raspberries threaded onto 4 bamboo skewers for garnish (optional)

■ Combine yogurt, tofu, raspberry preserves, banana, whey protein powder, and bee pollen in a blender or smoothie maker. Blend on high speed for 45 seconds or until mixture is puréed and smooth. Add raspberries and frozen yogurt, and blend on high speed again until mixture is smooth. Serve immediately, garnished with raspberries, if desired.

■ **YIELD:** Four 1-cup (235-ml) servings

BETTER FOR B6
BANANA DATE SMOOTHIE

BETTER FOR B6
BANANA DATE SMOOTHIE

Your immune system needs vitamin B6 to keep the lymphoid organs healthy and producing white blood cells, and bananas are high in this water-soluble vitamin. In addition, dates contain a fair amount of iron, and their succulent flavor is the perfect foil for the subtle banana.

   1 container (8 ounces or 225 g) banana low-fat yogurt
   ½ cup (120 ml) silken tofu
   2 cups (300 g) sliced banana
   1 cup (175 g) firmly packed pitted dried dates, diced
   2 tablespoons (30 ml) flaxseed oil
   2 tablespoons (30 g) bee pollen
   ½ cup (70 g) vanilla frozen yogurt
   2 tablespoons (20 g) finely chopped pitted dried dates
      for garnish (optional)

■ Combine yogurt, tofu, bananas, dates, flaxseed oil, and bee pollen in a blender or smoothie maker. Blend on high speed for 45 seconds or until mixture is puréed and smooth. Add frozen yogurt, and blend on high speed again until mixture is smooth. Serve immediately, garnished with chopped dates, if desired.

■ **YIELD:** Four 1-cup (235-ml) servings

FOLATE-FILLED
TROPICAL BANANA SMOOTHIE

FOLATE-FILLED
TROPICAL BANANA SMOOTHIE

Folate, which is important to maintaining your red blood cell production, is easy to find in legumes like lentils, but it's far more difficult to get a sufficient quantity from fruit. Papaya is one of the exceptions. It has a sweet flavor, a ton of vitamin C, and when joined with creamy banana and flavorful coconut, it makes a great smoothie.

- ¾ cup (175 ml) chilled papaya nectar
- ½ cup (120 ml) chilled light coconut milk
- ½ cup (120 ml) silken tofu
- 1 cup (175 g) diced papaya
- ½ cup (40 g) fresh shredded coconut
- 2 tablespoons (30 g) bee pollen
- 1½ cups (225 g) banana slices, frozen
- 8 mango cubes for garnish (optional)

■ Combine papaya nectar, coconut milk, tofu, papaya, coconut, and bee pollen in a blender or smoothie maker. Blend on high speed for 45 seconds or until mixture is puréed and smooth. Add banana slices, and blend on high speed again until mixture is smooth. Serve immediately, garnished with mango spears, if desired.

■ **YIELD:** Four 1-cup (235-ml) servings

CHOLESTEROL LOWERING MEXICAN CHOCOLATE BANANA SMOOTHIE

CHOLESTEROL LOWERING MEXICAN CHOCOLATE BANANA SMOOTHIE

Mexicans were the first to appreciate the wonders of hot chocolate, and their version is made with almonds and cinnamon. In addition to supplying a high content of vitamin E, which protects cell membranes against free radicals, and manganese, which helps your body metabolize fatty acids, almonds serve to prevent a rise in blood sugar after eating.

1 cup (235 ml) chocolate soy milk
½ cup (120 ml) silken tofu
1 cup (150 g) shelled almonds, not skinned
½ cup (50 g) chopped dark chocolate
2 tablespoons (30 ml) flaxseed oil
½ teaspoon (1.2 g) ground cinnamon
2 cups (300 g) banana slices, frozen
2 tablespoons (12.5 g) grated chocolate for garnish (optional)

■ Combine soy milk, tofu, almonds, chocolate, flaxseed oil, and cinnamon in a blender or smoothie maker. Blend on high speed for 45 seconds or until mixture is puréed and smooth. Add banana slices, and blend on high speed again until mixture is smooth. Serve immediately, garnished with grated chocolate, if desired.

■ **YIELD:** Four 1-cup (235-ml) servings

GUILT-FREE
BANANA CHOCOLATE SMOOTHIE

Great news for chocoholics: Dark chocolate contains the same heart-healthy flavonoids as red wine, so it, too, can help lower our cholesterol. In fact, one Dutch study showed that chocolate contains four times the amount of catechins as tea!

1½ cups (355 ml) chocolate soy milk
3 ounces (85 g) chopped dark chocolate
3 tablespoons (45 g) cocoa powder, preferably Dutch-processed
2 tablespoons (30 g) bee pollen
2 tablespoons (30 ml) flaxseed oil
2 cups (300 g) sliced banana
1 cup (140 g) chocolate frozen yogurt
2 tablespoons (15 g) shaved chocolate for garnish (optional)

■ Combine soy milk, chopped chocolate, cocoa powder, bee pollen, flaxseed oil, and banana in a blender or smoothie maker. Blend on high speed for 45 seconds or until mixture is puréed and smooth. Add frozen yogurt, and blend on high speed again until mixture is smooth. Serve immediately, garnished with chocolate shavings, if desired.

■ **YIELD:** Four 1-cup (235-ml) servings

CALMING TRYPTOPHAN SESAME CHOCOLATE BANANA SMOOTHIE

CALMING TRYPTOPHAN SESAME CHOCOLATE BANANA SMOOTHIE

The precursor of serotonin, tryptophan has a calming effect that can lead to relaxation and sleep. Sesame seeds and tofu are good sources of tryptophan and are packed with immune-boosting nutrients.

> 1 cup (235 ml) chocolate soy milk
> ½ cup (120 ml) silken tofu
> ⅓ cup (80 g) tahini
> ¼ cup (32 g) whey protein powder
> ¼ cup (30 g) sesame seeds
> 2 tablespoons (28 ml) chocolate syrup
> ¼ teaspoon (1 ml) pure vanilla extract
> 2 cups (300 g) banana slices, frozen
> 2 tablespoons (15 g) toasted sesame seeds (optional)

■ Combine soy milk, tofu, tahini, whey protein powder, sesame seeds, chocolate syrup, and vanilla extract in a blender or smoothie maker. Blend on high speed for 45 seconds or until mixture is puréed and smooth. Add banana slices, and blend on high speed again until mixture is smooth. Serve immediately, garnished with sesame seeds, if desired.

■ **YIELD:** Four 1-cup (235-ml) servings

FIBER-FILLED
BANANA COLADA SMOOTHIE

FIBER-FILLED
BANANA COLADA SMOOTHIE

There is a belief that foods that grow from the same soil taste good when eaten together, and the combination of tropical pineapple and coconut validates this theory. These fruits have wonderfully complementary flavors, and they are both high in fiber, a necessary part of a healthy diet. Bananas are added for their creamy texture and because they are rich in potassium.

- 1 cup (235 ml) light coconut milk
- 1 cup (155 g) diced pineapple
- ⅓ cup (25 g) lightly packed shredded unsweetened coconut
- ¼ cup (32 g) whey protein powder
- 2 tablespoons (30 g) bee pollen
- ½ teaspoon (2.5 ml) pure rum extract
- 2 cups (300 g) banana slices, frozen
- 2 tablespoons (6 g) grated coconut for garnish (optional)

■ Combine coconut milk, pineapple, coconut, whey protein powder, bee pollen, and rum extract in a blender or smoothie maker. Blend on high speed for 45 seconds or until mixture is puréed and smooth. Add banana slices, and blend on high speed again until mixture is smooth. Serve immediately, garnished with grated coconut, if desired.

■ **YIELD:** Four 1-cup (235-ml) servings

MARVELOUS MANGANESE VERY BERRY BANANA SMOOTHIE

Manganese is important for keeping bones healthy, so when flavorful raspberries and blackberries add their manganese-rich content to this nondairy smoothie—made creamy with bananas—it's a surefire winner.

½ cup (120 ml) plain soy milk
½ cup (120 ml) silken tofu
½ cup (70 g) blackberries
½ cup (60 g) raspberries
½ cup (85 g) strawberries, hulled and sliced
¼ cup (32 g) whey protein powder
2 cups (300 g) banana slices, frozen
4 strawberry fans for garnish (optional)

▨ Combine soy milk, tofu, blackberries, raspberries, strawberries, and whey protein powder in a blender or smoothie maker. Blend on high speed for 45 seconds or until mixture is puréed and smooth. Add banana slices, and blend on high speed again until mixture is smooth. Serve immediately, garnished with strawberry fans, if desired.

▨ **YIELD:** Four 1-cup (235-ml) servings

SUPER SELENIUM
BANANA BRAZIL NUT SMOOTHIE

SUPER SELENIUM
BANANA BRAZIL NUT SMOOTHIE

Brazil nuts have about 2,500 times as much selenium as any other nut. Selenium is a trace mineral with powerful antioxidant properties that has been proven to protect against heart disease and prostate cancer. Brazil nuts are also full of magnesium, fiber, and zinc.

2 cups (300 g) chopped Brazil nuts
1 cup (235 ml) silken tofu
3 tablespoons (60 g) honey
2 tablespoons (30 ml) flaxseed oil
½ teaspoon (1.2 g) ground cinnamon,
   plus extra for garnish (optional)
2 cups (300 g) banana slices, frozen

▪ Preheat oven to 350°F (180°C, or gas mark 4). Place Brazil nuts on a baking sheet, and bake for 5 to 7 minutes or until lightly browned. Remove nuts from oven, and allow to cool completely.

▪ Combine cooled nuts, tofu, honey, flaxseed oil, and cinnamon in a blender or smoothie maker. Blend on high speed for 45 seconds or until mixture is puréed and smooth. Add banana slices, and blend on high speed again until mixture is smooth. Serve immediately, garnished with a sprinkling of cinnamon, if desired.

▪ **YIELD:** Four 1-cup (235-ml) servings

THROAT-SOOTHING ALMOND HONEY BANANA SMOOTHIE

THROAT-SOOTHING ALMOND HONEY BANANA SMOOTHIE

Opera singers swear by honey to soothe sore throats before performances. This smoothie harnesses that power and adds other ingredients—such as manganese- and vitamin E-rich almonds—to boost the immune system (and help cure that sore throat even faster).

> 1 container (8 ounces or 225 g) plain low-fat yogurt
> ½ cup (120 ml) silken tofu
> 1 cup (150 g) shelled almonds, not skinned
> ¼ cup (85 g) honey
> ¼ cup (32 g) whey protein powder
> ¼ teaspoon (1.2 g) ground cinnamon
> ¼ teaspoon (1.2 ml) pure vanilla extract
> 2 cups (300 g) banana slices, frozen
> Sprinkle of ground cinnamon for garnish (optional)

■ Combine yogurt, tofu, almonds, honey, whey protein powder, cinnamon, and vanilla extract in a blender or smoothie maker. Blend on high speed for 45 seconds or until mixture is puréed and smooth. Add banana slices, and blend on high speed again until mixture is smooth. Serve immediately, garnished with a sprinkle of cinnamon, if desired.

■ **YIELD:** Four 1-cup (235-ml) servings

CHEERS FOR THE E-TEAM!
NUTTY ALMOND DATE SMOOTHIE

CHEERS FOR THE E-TEAM! NUTTY ALMOND DATE SMOOTHIE

Both crunchy almonds and sunflower seeds are loaded with vitamin E, which protects cell membranes. The combination of succulent dried dates, sweet applesauce, and a bit of ginger balances the nutty richness with fruity sparkle.

2 cups (490 g) chilled unsweetened applesauce
1 cup (150 g) shelled almonds, not skinned
½ cup (145 g) shelled sunflower seeds
¼ cup (32 g) whey protein powder
½ teaspoon (1 g) ground ginger
¼ teaspoon (1.2 ml) pure almond extract
1 cup (175 g) firmly packed pitted dried dates
4 green tea ice cubes
Sprinkle of ground cinnamon or cinnamon stick for garnish (optional)

■ Combine applesauce, almonds, sunflower seeds, whey protein powder, ginger, almond extract, and dates in a blender or smoothie maker. Blend on high speed for 45 seconds or until mixture is puréed and smooth. Add ice cubes, and blend on high speed again until mixture is smooth. Serve immediately, garnished with a sprinkle of cinnamon or cinnamon stick, if desired.

■ **YIELD:** Four 1-cup (235-ml) servings

UPPING THE IRON
MANGO MACADAMIA COCONUT
SMOOTHIE

UPPING THE IRON
MANGO MACADAMIA COCONUT SMOOTHIE

Hawaiian macadamia nuts, with their rich sweet flavor, are now easy to find, and this treat from the tropics is a good source of iron. When joined with mangoes, rich in both vitamin C and beta-carotene, this smoothie boosts your immune system and tastes like a vacation to a sunny climate.

   1 container (4 ounces or 112 g) peach low-fat yogurt
   ½ cup (120 ml) mango nectar
   ½ cup (120 ml) light coconut milk
   ¾ cup (110 g) roasted macadamia nuts
   ½ cup (40 g) shredded unsweetened dried coconut
   ¼ cup (32 g) whey protein powder
   2 tablespoons (30 g) bee pollen
   2 cups (350 g) diced mango, frozen
   4 mango spears for garnish (optional)

■ Combine yogurt, mango nectar, coconut milk, macadamia nuts, coconut, whey protein powder, and bee pollen in a blender or smoothie maker. Blend on high speed for 45 seconds or until mixture is puréed and smooth. Add mango, and blend on high speed again until mixture is smooth. Serve immediately, garnished with mango spears, if desired.

■ **YIELD:** Four 1-cup (235-ml) servings

MANGANESE-E
STRAWBERRY ALMOND SMOOTHIE

MANGANESE-E STRAWBERRY ALMOND SMOOTHIE

Almonds are a great source of two minerals—manganese and magnesium—as well as vitamin E, and the vitamin C-rich strawberries add color and sweetness to this smoothie.

1 container (8 ounces or 225 g) strawberry low-fat yogurt
½ cup (120 ml) silken tofu
¼ cup (80 g) fruit-only strawberry preserves
1 cup (150 g) shelled almonds, not skinned
¼ cup (32 g) whey protein powder
2 tablespoons (30 ml) flaxseed oil
1½ cups (220 g) strawberries, frozen
4 strawberry fans for garnish (optional)

■ Combine yogurt, tofu, strawberry preserves, almonds, whey protein powder, and flaxseed oil in a blender or smoothie maker. Blend on high speed for 45 seconds or until mixture is puréed and smooth. Add strawberries, and blend on high speed again until mixture is smooth. Serve immediately, garnished with strawberry fans, if desired.

■ **YIELD:** Four 1-cup (235-ml) servings

MINERAL MADNESS CARROT, PINEAPPLE, BRAZIL NUT SMOOTHIE

MINERAL MADNESS
CARROT, PINEAPPLE, BRAZIL NUT SMOOTHIE

Juicy pineapple is a great source of manganese, and buttery-flavored Brazil nuts are super-rich in selenium.

1 cup (150 g) chopped Brazil nuts
¾ cup (175 ml) chilled carrot juice
1 medium carrot, scrubbed, and cut into ½-inch (1-cm) slices
⅓ cup (80 ml) silken tofu
¼ cup (32 g) whey protein power
2 tablespoons (30 ml) flaxseed oil
¾ teaspoon (1.5 g) ground cinnamon
1½ cups (250 g) pineapple cubes, frozen
½ cup (70 g) vanilla frozen yogurt
4 pineapple spears for garnish (optional)

■ Preheat oven to 350°F (180°C, or gas mark 4). Place Brazil nuts on a baking sheet, and bake for 5 to 7 minutes or until lightly browned. Remove nuts from oven, and allow to cool completely.

■ Combine Brazil nuts, carrot juice, carrot, tofu, whey protein powder, flaxseed oil, and cinnamon in a blender or smoothie maker. Blend on high speed for 45 seconds or until mixture is puréed and smooth. Add pineapple and frozen yogurt, and blend on high speed again until mixture is smooth. Serve immediately, garnished with pineapple spears, if desired.

■ **YIELD:** Four 1-cup (235-ml) servings

FIBER FANTASTIC
MAPLE DATE NUT SMOOTHIE

Maple syrup, like honey, adds nutrients as well as sweetness to smoothies. This thickened sap from maple trees contains manganese and zinc, both of which are necessary for a healthy immune system.

> 1 cup (235 ml) plain soy milk
> ¼ cup (60 ml) pure maple syrup
> 1 cup (175 g) firmly packed pitted dried dates, diced
> ¾ cup (115 g) chopped Brazil nuts
> 1 sweet eating apple (such as McIntosh or Red Delicious),
>   cored, and diced
> ¼ cup (32 g) whey protein powder
> 2 tablespoons (30 ml) flaxseed oil
> 4 green tea ice cubes
> ½ cup (70 g) vanilla frozen yogurt
> 4 apple slices for garnish (optional)

■ Combine soy milk, maple syrup, dates, Brazil nuts, apple, whey protein powder, and flaxseed oil in a blender or smoothie maker. Blend on high speed for 45 seconds or until mixture is puréed and smooth. Add ice cubes and frozen yogurt, and blend on high speed again until mixture is smooth. Serve immediately, garnished with apple slices, if desired.

■ **YIELD:** Four 1-cup (235-ml) servings

HEALING HONEY
PEANUT BANANA SMOOTHIE

HEALING HONEY
PEANUT BANANA SMOOTHIE

In addition to sweetening this smoothie, honey serves a role in boosting the immune system; It is one of the few sources of pinocembrin, an antioxidant. Honey is also a healing agent—during World War I, it was mixed with cod liver oil and used to dress wounds on the battlefield.

1 cup (235 ml) plain soy milk
½ cup (120 ml) silken tofu
¼ cup (85 g) honey
1 cup (145 g) shelled peanuts
¼ cup (60 g) shelled sunflower seeds
¼ cup (32 g) whey protein powder
½ teaspoon (1.2 g) ground cinnamon
½ teaspoon (2.5 ml) pure vanilla extract
2 cups (300 g) banana slices, frozen
Sprinkling of cinnamon for garnish (optional)

■ Combine soy milk, tofu, honey, peanuts, sunflower seeds, whey protein powder, cinnamon, and vanilla extract in a blender or smoothie maker. Blend on high speed for 45 seconds or until mixture is puréed and smooth. Add banana slices, and blend on high speed again until mixture is smooth. Serve immediately, garnished with a sprinkling of cinnamon, if desired.

■ **YIELD:** Four 1-cup (235-ml) servings

PROTEIN-POWERED PB&J SMOOTHIE

Contrary to their name, peanuts are actually a member of the legume family; they are botanically related to lentils and beans. They are a wonderful source of protein and contain high amounts of manganese and folate. Blended with vitamin C-rich strawberries, they create an excellent immune-boosting smoothie.

> 1 container (8 ounces or 225 g) strawberry low-fat yogurt
> 1 cup (235 ml) plain soy milk
> 1 cup (145 g) shelled peanuts
> ¼ cup (32 g) whey protein powder
> ¼ cup (80 g) fruit-only strawberry preserves
> 1½ cups (220 g) strawberries, frozen
> 4 strawberry fans for garnish (optional)

■ Combine yogurt, soy milk, peanuts, whey protein powder, and strawberry preserves in a blender or smoothie maker. Blend on high speed for 45 seconds or until mixture is puréed and smooth. Add strawberries, and blend on high speed again until mixture is smooth. Serve immediately, garnished with strawberry fans, if desired.

■ **YIELD:** Four 1-cup (235-ml) servings

PURPLE GOLD BLUEBERRY BLACKBERRY SMOOTHIE

PURPLE GOLD
BLUEBERRY BLACKBERRY SMOOTHIE

Blackberries are a treasure trove of manganese and zinc, and when you complement those nutrients with the powerhouse of antioxidants in blueberries, your richly colored and richly flavored smoothie becomes as good for your health as it is to drink!

> 1 container (8 ounces or 225 g) blueberry low-fat yogurt
> 1 cup (235 ml) unsweetened purple grape juice
> 2 tablespoons (30 g) bee pollen
> 1 tablespoon (15 ml) freshly squeezed lemon juice
> 1 cup (145 g) blueberries, frozen
> 1 cup (145 g) blackberries, frozen
> ½ cup (70 g) vanilla frozen yogurt
> 12 blackberries or blueberries threaded onto 4 bamboo skewers for garnish (optional)

■ Combine yogurt, grape juice, bee pollen, and lemon juice in a blender or smoothie maker. Blend on high speed for 45 seconds or until mixture is puréed and smooth. Add blueberries, blackberries, and frozen yogurt, and blend on high speed again until mixture is smooth. Serve immediately, garnished with fruit skewers, if desired.

■ **YIELD:** Four 1-cup (235-ml) servings

FLAVONOID FIESTA
APPLE BLUEBERRY SMOOTHIE

FLAVONOID FIESTA
APPLE BLUEBERRY SMOOTHIE

There is a synergistic relationship between flavonoids—the chemicals that give foods their color—and vitamin C: The flavonoids empower vitamin C to fight infection. Sweet apples and vibrant blueberries are both loaded with flavonoids, and when blended, they produce a luscious flavor and a lovely lavender color that make this smoothie a visually appealing taste treat.

- 1 container (8 ounces or 225 g) blueberry low-fat yogurt
- ½ cup (120 ml) chilled cloudy apple juice
- 1 sweet eating apple (such as McIntosh or Red Delicious), cored and diced
- ¼ cup (32 g) whey protein powder
- 1½ cups (220 g) blueberries, frozen
- 4 apple wedges for garnish (optional)

▧ Combine yogurt, apple juice, apple, and whey protein powder in a blender or smoothie maker. Blend on high speed for 45 seconds or until mixture is puréed and smooth. Add blueberries, and blend on high speed again until mixture is smooth. Serve immediately, garnished with an apple wedge, if desired.

▧ **YIELD:** Four 1-cup (235-ml) servings

PROTEIN-PACKED BERRY GOOD BLUEBERRY SMOOTHIE

PROTEIN-PACKED
BERRY GOOD BLUEBERRY SMOOTHIE

Like most dairy products, cream cheese is a good source of vitamin A, calcium, and protein. When joined with blueberries, a stellar antioxidant, the result is a delicious drink that tastes like cheesecake.

1 container (8 ounces or 225 g) blueberry low-fat yogurt
1 package (3 ounces or 85 g) cream cheese, cut into ½-inch (1-cm) pieces
½ cup (120 ml) silken tofu
¼ cup (80 g) fruit-only blueberry preserves
¼ cup (42 g) dried blueberries
¼ cup (32 g) whey protein powder
2½ cups (365 g) blueberries, frozen
16 blueberries threaded onto 4 bamboo skewers for garnish (optional)

■ Combine yogurt, cream cheese, tofu, blueberry preserves, dried blueberries, and whey protein powder in a blender or smoothie maker. Blend on high speed for 45 seconds or until mixture is puréed and smooth. Add blueberries, and blend on high speed again until mixture is smooth. Serve immediately, garnished with blueberry skewers, if desired.

■ **YIELD:** Four 1-cup (235-ml) servings

C-SUPER
MANGO PINEAPPLE SMOOTHIE

C-SUPER
MANGO PINEAPPLE SMOOTHIE

You can never get too much of the all-important antioxidant vitamin C. That said, it is best taken at various intervals throughout the day because your body excretes what it does not need at the moment, making it impossible to store any for the future. These two tropical treats—mango and pineapple—deliver plenty of this necessary nutrient.

1 container (8 ounces or 225 g) plain low-fat yogurt
½ cup (120 ml) silken tofu
1½ cups (260 g) diced mango
½ cup (40 g) unsweetened dried shredded coconut
2 tablespoons (30 g) bee pollen
½ teaspoon (2.5 ml) pure coconut extract
1 cup (155 g) diced pineapple, frozen
4 pineapple or mango spears for garnish (optional)

■ Combine yogurt, tofu, mango, coconut, bee pollen, and coconut extract in a blender or smoothie maker. Blend on high speed for 45 seconds or until mixture is puréed and smooth. Add pineapple, and blend on high speed again until mixture is smooth. Serve immediately, garnished with pineapple spears, if desired.

■ **YIELD:** Four 1-cup (235-ml) servings

TROPICAL TEAMWORK
PAPAYA PINEAPPLE SMOOTHIE

TROPICAL TEAMWORK
PAPAYA PINEAPPLE SMOOTHIE

Pineapple, the fruit with the highest content of manganese, is a good source of vitamin C, and papaya is almost over-the-top when it comes to its vitamin-C level. Together, these two fruits add up to a delicious smoothie.

> 1 container (8 ounces or 225 g) plain low-fat yogurt
> ½ cup (120 ml) silken tofu
> ½ cup (120 ml) chilled papaya nectar
> 2 tablespoons (30 g) bee pollen
> 1 cup (140 g) diced papaya
> 1½ cups (225 g) peach slices, frozen
> 4 pineapple spears for garnish (optional)

■ Combine yogurt, tofu, papaya nectar, bee pollen, and papaya in a blender or smoothie maker. Blend on high speed for 45 seconds or until mixture is puréed and smooth. Add peach slices, and blend on high speed again until mixture is smooth. Serve immediately, garnished with pineapple spears, if desired.

■ **YIELD:** Four 1-cup (235-ml) servings

CUP OF COPPER
SESAME PAPAYA SMOOTHIE

Sesame seeds are a great source of copper, a nutrient we need to help our bodies utilize iron and fight free radicals. The subtle sesame flavor melds wonderfully with vitamin C-rich papaya in this smoothie.

1 cup (235 ml) chilled papaya nectar
½ cup (120 ml) silken tofu
⅓ cup (80 g) tahini
2 tablespoons (30 g) bee pollen
2 cups (350 g) diced papaya, frozen
4 papaya spears for garnish (optional)

■ Combine papaya nectar, tofu, tahini, and bee pollen in a blender or smoothie maker. Blend on high speed for 45 seconds or until mixture is puréed and smooth. Add papaya pieces, and blend on high speed again until mixture is smooth. Serve immediately. Garnish with papaya spears, if desired.

■ **YIELD:** Four 1-cup (235-ml) servings

CACHE OF CATECHINS
GREEN TEA PAPAYA SMOOTHIE

A study published in the *Journal of Allergy and Clinical Immunology* found that the antioxidants found in green tea are more effective than either vitamin C or vitamin E at protecting cells and DNA from free-radical damage. In this smoothie, green tea's flavor forms a subtle background for the vivid tropical taste of mineral-rich papaya.

> ½ cup (120 ml) chilled papaya nectar
> 1 tablespoon (15 ml) freshly squeezed lime juice
> 2 cups (350 g) diced papaya
> ¼ cup (32 g) whey protein powder
> 2 tablespoons (30 g) bee pollen
> 8 green tea ice cubes
> 4 papaya and 4 lime wedges for garnish (optional)

▨ Combine papaya nectar, lime juice, papaya, whey protein powder, and bee pollen in a blender or smoothie maker. Blend on high speed for 45 seconds or until mixture is puréed and smooth. Add ice cubes, and blend on high speed again until mixture is smooth. Serve immediately, garnished with papaya spears, if desired.

▨ **YIELD:** Four 1-cup (235-ml) servings

TENDER FOR THE TUMMY GINGER PAPAYA SMOOTHIE

Ginger contains valuable minerals, including potassium, magnesium, and copper, and has many curative properties: It calms the stomach, mitigates nausea, and has anti-inflammatory properties that help with arthritis pain. It also adds fantastic flavor to this smoothie made with vitamin C- and folate-filled papaya.

1 cup (235 ml) chilled papaya nectar
1 container (8 ounces or 225 g) peach low-fat yogurt
½ cup (120 ml) silken tofu
¼ cup (32 g) whey protein powder
3 tablespoons (24 g) crystallized ginger
2 cups (280 g) papaya cubes, frozen
4 papaya spears for garnish (optional)

■ Combine papaya nectar, yogurt, tofu, whey protein powder, and crystallized ginger in a blender or smoothie maker. Blend on high speed for 45 seconds or until mixture is puréed and smooth. Add papaya cubes, and blend on high speed again until mixture is smooth. Serve immediately, garnished with papaya spears, if desired.

■ **YIELD:** Four 1-cup (235-ml) servings

MULTI-MINERAL CANTALOUPE BLACKBERRY SMOOTHIE

MULTI-MINERAL
CANTALOUPE BLACKBERRY SMOOTHIE

Blackberries share many antioxidant qualities with their visual cousin, the blueberry, but they are also an excellent source of such important immune-boosting minerals as magnesium, manganese, and zinc. When combined with low-calorie cantaloupe, which is loaded with vitamin A and vitamin C, you have a very healthful and delicious smoothie.

1 container (8 ounces or 225 g) vanilla low-fat yogurt
½ cup (120 ml) silken tofu
2 cups (310 g) diced cantaloupe
¼ cup (80 g) fruit-only blackberry preserves
¼ cup (32 g) whey protein power
1½ cups (220 g) blackberries, frozen
4 blackberries for garnish (optional)

■ Combine yogurt, tofu, cantaloupe, blackberry preserves, and whey protein powder in a blender or smoothie maker. Blend on high speed for 45 seconds or until mixture is puréed and smooth. Add blackberries, and blend on high speed again until mixture is smooth. Serve immediately, garnished with berry skewers, if desired.

■ **YIELD:** Four 1-cup (235-ml) servings

C-POWER
CANTALOUPE CITRUS SMOOTHIE

C-POWER
CANTALOUPE CITRUS SMOOTHIE

One whole cantaloupe delivers more vitamin A and vitamin C than you need in an entire day—talk about a food superstar! When its rich flavor is joined with the sparkle of other vitamin C-rich citrus fruits like grapefruit and orange, your smoothie is armed and ready to protect you from harm.

1 cup (235 ml) freshly squeezed orange juice
½ cup (120 ml) freshly squeezed grapefruit juice, preferably from a red grapefruit
¼ cup (32 g) whey protein powder
2 tablespoons (30 g) bee pollen
1 tablespoon (15 ml) freshly squeezed lemon or lime juice
2 cups (320 g) cantaloupe cubes, frozen
4 orange slices for garnish (optional)

▦ Combine orange juice, grapefruit juice, whey protein powder, bee pollen, and lemon or lime juice in a blender or smoothie maker. Blend on high speed for 20 seconds or until mixture is puréed and smooth. Add cantaloupe cubes, and blend on high speed again until mixture is smooth. Serve immediately, garnished with orange slices, if desired.

▦ **YIELD:** Four 1-cup (235-ml) servings

C-PRISINGLY DELICIOUS
CITRUS STRAWBERRY SMOOTHIE

C-PRISINGLY DELICIOUS
CITRUS STRAWBERRY SMOOTHIE

Sweet and sour flavors balance one another well in this smoothie
filled with vitamin C-rich fruits.

> 2 navel oranges & 1 red grapefruit
> 1 cup (235 ml) freshly squeezed orange juice
> ⅔ cup (150 ml) freshly squeezed grapefruit juice
> ½ cup (160 g) fruit-only strawberry preserves
> ⅓ cup (75 g) shelled sunflower seeds
> ¼ cup (32 g) whey protein powder
> 1½ cups (220 g) strawberries, frozen
> 4 fresh strawberry fans for garnish (optional)

■ Peel oranges and grapefruit, and slice off white pith. Cut
around sides of sections to release segments from remaining pith.
Cut into ½-inch (1-cm) dice.

■ Combine oranges, grapefruit, orange juice, grapefruit juice,
strawberry preserves, sunflower seeds, and whey protein powder in
a blender or smoothie maker. Blend on high speed for 45 seconds
or until mixture is puréed and smooth. Add strawberries, and blend
on high speed again until mixture is smooth. Serve immediately,
garnished with strawberry fans, if desired.

■ **YIELD:** Four 1-cup (235-ml) servings

PHENOL-FILLED
PRUNE WHIP SMOOTHIE

Prunes are the dried form of plums, and both are high in phenols, which have long been touted for their antioxidant function. Phenols have been shown to inhibit oxygen-based damage to fats, including the fats that comprise a substantial proportion of our brain cells.

 1 container (8 ounces or 225 g) vanilla low-fat yogurt
 ½ cup (120 ml) silken tofu
 ¾ cup (130 g) unsulfured pitted prunes
 ½ cup (122 g) shelled sunflower seeds
 ¼ cup (32 g) whey protein powder
 2 fresh plums, pitted and sliced
 4 green tea ice cubes
 4 plum slices for garnish (optional)

▓ Combine yogurt, tofu, prunes, sunflower seeds, whey protein powder, and plums in a blender or smoothie maker. Blend on high speed for 45 seconds or until mixture is puréed and smooth. Add ice cubes, and blend on high speed again until mixture is smooth. Serve immediately, garnished with plum slices, if desired.

▓ **YIELD:** Four 1-cup (235-ml) servings

SUBLIMELY STRAWBERRY C-LOADED SMOOTHIE

If you prefer smoothies with one dominant flavor rather than a blend of tastes, this is the recipe for you. Strawberries are not only a superb source of vitamin C, but they also contain a high amount of anthocyanin pigments, which give strawberries their rich red color and help to protect cell structures against oxidative damage.

1 container (8 ounces or 225 g) strawberry low-fat yogurt
¾ cup (175 ml) plain soy milk
½ cup (120 ml) silken tofu
¼ cup (32 g) whey protein powder
¼ cup (80 g) fruit-only strawberry preserves
2 cups (290 g) strawberries, frozen
4 whole strawberries or strawberry fans for garnish (optional)

▨ Combine yogurt, soy milk, tofu, whey protein powder, and preserves in a blender or smoothie maker. Blend on high speed for 20 seconds or until mixture is puréed and smooth. Add strawberries, and blend on high speed again until mixture is smooth. Serve immediately, garnished with a strawberry fan, if desired.

▨ **YIELD:** Four 1-cup (235-ml) servings

PERKY AND C-LICIOUS WATERMELON STRAWBERRY SMOOTHIE

PERKY AND C-LICIOUS
WATERMELON STRAWBERRY SMOOTHIE

When watermelon is paired with two forms of strawberries, you get a vitamin C-filled smoothie with a vivid pink color and a delicious fruity flavor.

2 cups (300 g) seedless diced watermelon, chilled
½ cup (120 ml) silken tofu
¼ cup (80 g) fruit-only strawberry preserves
2 tablespoons (30 g) bee pollen
1 tablespoon (15 ml) freshly squeezed lemon juice
1½ cups (220 g) strawberries, frozen
½ cup (70 g) vanilla frozen yogurt
4 watermelon wedges or strawberry fans for garnish (optional)

■ Combine watermelon, tofu, strawberry preserves, bee pollen, and lemon juice in a blender or smoothie maker. Blend on high speed for 45 seconds or until mixture is puréed and smooth. Add strawberries and frozen yogurt, and blend on high speed again until mixture is smooth. Serve immediately, garnished with watermelon wedges or strawberry fans, if desired.

■ **YIELD:** Four 1-cup (235-ml) servings

SAY C
STRAWBERRY MANGO BANANA
SMOOTHIE

SAY C
STRAWBERRY MANGO BANANA SMOOTHIE

Aromatic sweet mangoes and luscious strawberries are both excellent sources of vitamin C, a powerful antioxidant the body uses to fight infection. In this blushing pink smoothie, they team up with creamy banana, which is high in the potassium your body needs to maintain normal blood pressure.

> ¾ cup (175 ml) chilled mango nectar
> ½ cup (120 ml) silken tofu
> 1 cup (145 g) strawberries
> 1 cup (175 g) diced mango
> ¼ cup (32 g) whey protein powder
> 2 tablespoons (30 g) bee pollen
> 1 cup (150 g) banana slices, frozen
> 8 mango spears for garnish (optional)

■ Combine mango nectar, tofu, strawberries, mango, whey protein powder, and bee pollen in a blender or smoothie maker. Blend on high speed for 45 seconds or until mixture is puréed and smooth. Add banana slices, and blend on high speed again until mixture is smooth. Serve immediately, garnished with mango spears, if desired.

■ **YIELD:** Four 1-cup (235-ml) servings

E-LICIOUS
PASTEL PUNCH SMOOTHIE

E-LICIOUS
PASTEL PUNCH SMOOTHIE

Vitamin E, a key nutrient found in crunchy sunflower seeds, neutralizes free radicals that might otherwise damage cell membranes and other fat-containing structures. This smoothie also features a healthy rainbow of sweet and delicious fruits.

1 cup (235 ml) purple grape juice
½ cup (120 ml) pomegranate juice or pomegranate-blueberry juice
½ cup (120 ml) silken tofu
½ cup (112 g) shelled sunflower seeds
1 container (4 ounces or 112 g) blueberry low-fat yogurt
1 medium banana, peeled and sliced
½ cup (75 g) blueberries, frozen
½ cup (75 g) raspberries, frozen
½ cup (70 g) vanilla frozen yogurt
16 fresh blueberries or raspberries threaded onto 4 skewers for garnish (optional)

■ Combine grape juice, pomegranate juice, tofu, sunflower seeds, yogurt, and banana in a blender or smoothie maker. Blend on high speed for 45 seconds or until mixture is puréed and smooth. Add blueberries, raspberries, and frozen yogurt, and blend on high speed again until mixture is smooth. Serve immediately, garnished with berry skewers, if desired.

■ **YIELD:** Four 1-cup (235-ml) servings

VITAMIN A ODYSSEY
APRICOT PEACH SMOOTHIE

VITAMIN A ODYSSEY
APRICOT PEACH SMOOTHIE

The bright orange color of apricots and peaches should serve as your clue that they are both good sources of beta-carotene, which helps protect your cells from free radicals, and lycopene, which may lower cholesterol and help prevent heart disease.

> 1 cup (235 ml) chilled apricot nectar
> ½ cup (120 ml) silken tofu
> ½ cup (65 g) unsulfured dried apricots
> 1½ cups (255 g) peach slices, frozen
> ½ cup (70 g) vanilla frozen yogurt
> 4 peach wedges for garnish (optional)

■ Combine apricot nectar, tofu, and dried apricots in a blender or smoothie maker. Blend on high speed for 45 seconds or until mixture is puréed and smooth. Add peach slices and frozen yogurt, and blend on high speed again until mixture is smooth. Serve immediately, garnished with peach wedges, if desired.

■ **YIELD:** Four 1-cup (235-ml) servings

GREEN MACHINE
KIWI HONEYDEW SMOOTHIE

If you're looking for antioxidants, look no further than bright green kiwi-fruit, which contain a phytonutrient that helps to protect the DNA in human cells from oxygen-related damage. Moreover, they are a fabulous source of vitamin C. Here, the fruit's green color is enhanced by luscious, low-calorie honeydew melon, in a drink with a light, lemony taste.

> 1 container (8 ounces or 225 g) lemon low-fat yogurt
> ½ cup (120 ml) silken tofu
> 6 kiwifruit, peeled and diced
> 1½ cups (255 g) diced honeydew melon
> ¼ cup (32 g) whey protein powder
> ½ cup (75 g) lemon sorbet
> 4 kiwi slices for garnish (optional)

■ Combine yogurt, tofu, kiwi, honeydew melon, and whey protein powder in a blender or smoothie maker. Blend on high speed for 45 seconds or until mixture is puréed and smooth. Add lemon sorbet, and blend on high speed again until mixture is smooth. Serve immediately, garnished with kiwi slices, if desired.

■ **YIELD:** Four 1-cup (235-ml) servings

PRIMING THE PUMP
CITRUS GREEN TEA SMOOTHIE

Green tea contains an antigen that does not fully activate the body's T-cells, but it does keep them in a state of readiness so that when bacteria arrive, the cells are ready to fight.

> 4 navel oranges
> 2 large red or pink grapefruit
> ¼ cup (80 g) fruit-only orange marmalade
> 2 tablespoons (30 ml) flaxseed oil
> 2 tablespoons (30 g) bee pollen
> 8 green tea ice cubes
> 4 orange slices or peels for garnish (optional)

■ Peel oranges and grapefruit, and slice off white pith. Cut around sides of sections to release segments from remaining pith. Cut into ½-inch (1-cm) dice.

■ Combine orange and grapefruit sections, orange marmalade, flaxseed oil, and bee pollen in a blender or smoothie maker. Blend on high speed for 45 seconds or until mixture is puréed and smooth. Add ice cubes, and blend on high speed again until mixture is smooth. Serve immediately, garnished with orange slices, if desired.

■ **YIELD:** Four 1-cup (235-ml) servings

RAVES FOR RESVERATROL
GRAPE BLUEBERRY SMOOTHIE

RAVES FOR RESVERATROL GRAPE BLUEBERRY SMOOTHIE

Flavonoids, which give red grapes and blueberries their vibrant colors, are phytonutrients that are extremely helpful to the body. Grapes, along with blueberries, peanuts, and red wine, contain resveratrol, an antioxidant that may help reduce the risk of heart disease.

 1 cup (235 ml) chilled purple grape juice
 ½ cup (120 ml) silken tofu
 ¼ cup (32 g) whey protein powder
 2 tablespoons (40 g) fruit-only grape jelly
 1½ cups (220 g) blueberries
 1½ cups (240 g) red seedless grapes, frozen
 12 red seedless grapes threaded onto 4 toothpicks for
   garnish (optional)

Combine grape juice, tofu, whey protein powder, grape jelly, and blueberries in a blender or smoothie maker. Blend on high speed for 45 seconds or until mixture is puréed and smooth. Add grapes, and blend on high speed again until mixture is smooth. Serve immediately, garnished with grape skewers, if desired.

YIELD: Four 1-cup (235-ml) servings

ANTIOXIDANT-ABUNDANT GRAPE KIWI SMOOTHIE

ANTIOXIDANT-ABUNDANT GRAPE KIWI SMOOTHIE

Not only are grapes a great source of immune-boosting manganese, but their skins contain resveratrol, a powerful antioxidant. So when you combine grapes with kiwifruit—a leader in vitamin-C content—your immune system gets double the boost.

1 cup (235 ml) chilled white grape juice
½ cup (120 ml) silken tofu
6 kiwifruit, peeled and diced
¼ cup (32 g) whey protein powder
2 cups (320 g) green grapes, frozen
4 kiwi slices for garnish (optional)

■ Combine grape juice, tofu, kiwifruit, and whey protein powder in a blender or smoothie maker. Blend on high speed for 45 seconds or until mixture is puréed and smooth. Add grapes, and blend on high speed again until mixture is smooth. Serve immediately, garnished with kiwi slices, if desired.

■ **YIELD:** Four 1-cup (235-ml) servings

ENZYME-ACTIVATING MANGO RASPBERRY SMOOTHIE

Raspberries are a superb source of manganese, an important mineral that activates the enzymes responsible for using other key nutrients to boost your immune system. Raspberries' succulent flavor is a great match for the aromatic richness of mango, which is high in antioxidant vitamin C.

1 container (8 ounces or 225 g) raspberry low-fat yogurt
½ cup (120 ml) chilled mango nectar
¾ cup (95 g) raspberries
¼ cup (32 g) whey protein powder
2 tablespoons (30 g) bee pollen
1½ cups (250 g) mango slices, frozen
½ cup (70 g) raspberry sorbet
4 peach or mango slices for garnish (optional)

▨ Combine yogurt, mango nectar, raspberries, whey protein powder, and bee pollen in a blender or smoothie maker. Blend on high speed for 45 seconds or until mixture is puréed and smooth. Add mango slices and sorbet, and blend on high speed again until mixture is smooth. Serve immediately, garnished with peach or mango slices, if desired.

▨ **YIELD:** Four 1-cup (235-ml) servings

ELLAGIC EXCITEMENT
RASPBERRY BANANA SMOOTHIE

ELLAGIC EXCITEMENT RASPBERRY BANANA SMOOTHIE

Many health food stores sell ellagic acid, which has antiviral, anti-bacterial, and anticarcinogenic properties, but raspberries are your naturally delicious, go-to food source for this powerful antioxidant phytonutrient. In addition, the flavonoids that give raspberries their red color are an immunity booster, and raspberries and bananas are both good sources of fiber.

- 1 container (8 ounces or 225 g) raspberry low-fat yogurt
- ½ cup (120 ml) silken tofu
- ¼ cup (80 g) fruit-only raspberry preserves
- ¼ cup (32 g) whey protein powder
- 2 tablespoons (30 g) bee pollen
- 2 cups (300 g) sliced banana
- 1½ cups (190 g) raspberries, frozen
- 12 raspberries threaded onto 4 toothpicks for garnish (optional)

■ Combine yogurt, tofu, raspberry preserves, whey protein powder, bee pollen, and banana in a blender or smoothie maker. Blend on high speed for 45 seconds or until mixture is puréed and smooth. Add raspberries, and blend on high speed again until mixture is smooth. Serve immediately, garnished with raspberry skewers, if desired.

■ **YIELD:** Four 1-cup (235-ml) servings

BRIGHT EYES
ABSOLUTELY APRICOT SMOOTHIE

The beta-carotene that your body converts to vitamin A is important for regulating your immune system, as it helps the skin and mucous membranes function as a barrier to bacteria. The vitamin is also crucial for maintaining good vision because it promotes healthy surface linings in the eyes. Apricots are an excellent source of vitamin A, and when three different forms of this vivid orange fruit are combined into one smoothie, their succulent flavor is magnified.

1 cup (235 ml) chilled apricot nectar
½ cup (120 ml) silken tofu
1 cup (175 g) firmly packed dried apricot halves, diced
¼ cup (32 g) whey protein powder
1½ cups (250 g) apricot slices, frozen
½ cup (70 g) vanilla frozen yogurt
4 apricot slices for garnish (optional)

■ Combine apricot nectar, tofu, dried apricots, and whey protein powder in a blender or smoothie maker. Blend on high speed for 45 seconds or until mixture is puréed and smooth. Add frozen apricot slices and frozen yogurt, and blend on high speed again until mixture is smooth. Serve immediately, garnished with apricot slices, if desired.

■ **YIELD:** Four 1-cup (235-ml) servings

PHILLED WITH PHENOLS
PINEAPPLE PLUM SMOOTHIE

PHILLED WITH PHENOLS
PINEAPPLE PLUM SMOOTHIE

Plums and their dried-form, prunes, are high in phytonutrients, classified as phenols, and provide antioxidant muscle for your body. In addition, they contain iron, which is more readily absorbed when taken with vitamin C, a nutrient found in pineapple.

1 container (8 ounces or 225 g) plain low-fat yogurt
½ cup (120 ml) silken tofu
1½ cups (235 g) diced pineapple
¼ cup (32 g) whey protein powder
2 tablespoons (30 g) bee pollen
1 cup (165 g) diced plums, frozen
4 pineapple spears for garnish (optional)

■ Combine yogurt, tofu, pineapple, whey protein powder, and bee pollen in a blender or smoothie maker. Blend on high speed for 45 seconds or until mixture is puréed and smooth. Add plums, and blend on high speed again until mixture is smooth. Serve immediately, garnished with pineapple spears, if desired.

■ **YIELD:** Four 1-cup (235-ml) servings

BROMELAIN BONUS
GINGERED PINEAPPLE BANANA
SMOOTHIE

BROMELAIN BONUS
GINGERED PINEAPPLE BANANA
SMOOTHIE

In addition to being high in manganese and vitamin C, pineapple is rich in bromelain, an enzyme that aids in digestion and can reduce inflammation. Ginger is also known for its tummy-taming powers, so this luscious tropical smoothie is the one to make if intestinal distress is an issue.

1 cup (235 ml) chilled pineapple juice
½ cup (120 ml) silken tofu
¼ cup (55 g) crystallized ginger
¼ cup (32 g) whey protein powder
1 cup (155 g) diced pineapple
1 cup (150 g) banana slices, frozen
4 pineapple spears or pineapple leaves for garnish (optional)

▨ Combine pineapple juice, tofu, ginger, whey protein powder, and diced pineapple in a blender or smoothie maker. Blend on high speed for 45 seconds or until mixture is puréed and smooth. Add banana slices, and blend on high speed again until mixture is smooth. Serve immediately, garnished with pineapple spears or leaves, if desired.

▨ **YIELD:** Four 1-cup (235-ml) servings

BORON BONUS
CRUNCHY RAISIN SMOOTHIE

Boron may not receive a lot of play, but this trace mineral is vital to your health because it prevents bone loss, especially in post-menopausal women. Raisins are an excellent source of boron, and both raisins and their parent fruit—grapes—are very high in antioxidant phenols that boost your immune system.

1 cup (235 ml) plain soy milk
¾ cup (110 g) raisins
½ cup (112 g) shelled sunflower seeds
2 tablespoons (30 ml) flaxseed oil
½ teaspoon (2.5 ml) pure vanilla extract
¼ teaspoon (1.2 g) ground cinnamon
2 cups (320 g) seedless red grapes, frozen
¼ cup (55 g) granola
2 tablespoons (28 g) granola for garnish (optional)

■ Combine soy milk, raisins, sunflower seeds, flaxseed oil, vanilla extract, and cinnamon in a blender or smoothie maker. Blend on high speed for 45 seconds or until mixture is puréed and smooth. Add grapes, and blend on high speed again until mixture is smooth. Add granola, and pulse a few times to distribute it evenly. Serve immediately, garnished with additional granola, if desired.

■ **YIELD:** Four 1-cup (235-ml) servings

COLON-KIND
PEACHY CARROT SMOOTHIE

COLON-KIND
PEACHY CARROT SMOOTHIE

When carrots are blended into a smoothie with sweet peaches (in three forms), the result is a healthful orange whirl.

> 1 container (8 ounces or 225 g) peach low-fat yogurt
> ½ cup (120 ml) chilled carrot juice
> ½ cup (120 ml) chilled peach nectar
> 2 medium carrots, trimmed, scrubbed, and sliced
> 2 tablespoons (30 g) bee pollen
> 2 cups (340 g) peach slices, frozen
> 4 fresh peach slices for garnish (optional)

■ Combine yogurt, carrot juice, peach nectar, carrots, and bee pollen in a blender or smoothie maker. Blend on high speed for 45 seconds or until mixture is puréed and smooth. Add peaches, and blend on high speed again until mixture is smooth. Serve immediately, garnished with fresh peach slices, if desired.

■ **YIELD:** Four 1-cup (235-ml) servings

CELL-SUPPORTING GUACAMOLE SMOOTHIE

CELL-SUPPORTING GUACAMOLE SMOOTHIE

In this satisfying and savory smoothie, avocados take center stage, while the other flavors associated with this popular Mexican dip play supporting roles.

1 container (8 ounces or 225 g) plain nonfat yogurt
½ cup (120 ml) silken tofu
2 scallions, trimmed and sliced
4 ripe avocados, peeled and diced
1 small jalapeño or serrano chile pepper, seeds and ribs removed, and diced
2 tablespoons (30 ml) freshly squeezed lime juice
2 tablespoons (30 g) bee pollen
6 green tea ice cubes
4 tortilla chips for garnish (optional)

■ Combine yogurt, tofu, scallions, avocados, chile pepper, lime juice, and bee pollen in a blender or smoothie maker. Blend on high speed for 45 seconds or until mixture is puréed and smooth. Add ice cubes, and blend on high speed again until mixture is smooth. Serve immediately, garnished with tortilla chips, if desired.

■ **YIELD:** Four 1-cup (235-ml) servings

BLOOD-BOOSTING
GRAPEFRUIT AVOCADO SMOOTHIE

BLOOD-BOOSTING GRAPEFRUIT AVOCADO SMOOTHIE

A good source of fiber, potassium, and folate, avocados add richness to this purée of vitamin C-rich grapefruit and sweet raspberries.

2 red grapefruit
½ cup (120 ml) freshly squeezed orange juice
½ cup (120 ml) silken tofu
¼ cup (56 g) shelled sunflower seeds
2 ripe avocados, peeled and diced
½ cup (65 g) raspberries, frozen
4 green tea ice cubes
4 raspberries or grapefruit sections reserved for garnish (optional)

■ Peel grapefruit and slice off white pith. Cut around sides of sections to release segments from remaining pith. Reserve four sections, if using as garnish, and cut remaining grapefruit into ½-inch (1-cm) dice.

■ Combine grapefruit sections, orange juice, tofu, sunflower seeds, and avocados in a blender or smoothie maker. Blend on high speed for 45 seconds or until mixture is puréed and smooth. Add frozen raspberries and ice cubes, and blend on high speed again until mixture is smooth. Serve immediately, garnished with grapefruit sections, if desired.

■ **YIELD:** Four 1-cup (235-ml) servings

BETA-BLAST CANTALOUPE GAZPACHO SMOOTHIE

BETA-BLAST
CANTALOUPE GAZPACHO SMOOTHIE

Cantaloupe's orange color should be your clue that this low-calorie fruit is loaded with beta-carotene.

- 1 container (8 ounces or 225 g) plain nonfat yogurt
- ½ cup (120 ml) silken tofu
- ½ pound (225 g) orange tomatoes, cored, and cut into 1-inch (2.5-cm) cubes
- ½ small orange bell pepper, seeds and ribs removed, and diced
- 1 celery stalk, trimmed and sliced
- 1 small shallot, peeled and sliced
- 2 tablespoons (30 ml) cider vinegar
- 2 tablespoons (30 ml) flaxseed oil
- 2 cups (310 g) diced cantaloupe, frozen
- Salt and hot pepper sauce to taste
- 4 celery sprigs for garnish (optional)

■ Combine yogurt, tofu, tomatoes, bell pepper, celery, shallot, vinegar, and flaxseed oil in a blender or smoothie maker. Blend on high speed for 45 seconds or until mixture is puréed and smooth. Add cantaloupe, and blend on high speed again until mixture is smooth. Season to taste with salt and hot pepper sauce, and serve immediately, garnished with celery sprigs, if desired.

■ **YIELD:** Four 1-cup (235-ml) servings

TERRIFIC THIAMIN
HERBED TOMATO SMOOTHIE

TERRIFIC THIAMIN
HERBED TOMATO SMOOTHIE

Maintaining your body's energy supply is fundamental in keeping your immune system healthy, and that is where vitamin B1, commonly called thiamin, comes in. Sunflower seeds are a superb source of this key nutrient. The seeds add a crunchy texture to this savory smoothie that also delivers heart-protecting lycopene from the tomatoes.

1 cup (235 ml) chilled tomato juice
⅔ cup (150 g) shelled sunflower seeds
¼ cup (32 g) whey protein powder
1 tablespoon (15 ml) freshly squeezed lemon juice
½ cup (20 g) loosely packed fresh basil leaves
¼ cup (10 g) loosely packed fresh oregano leaves
¼ cup (15 g) loosely packed fresh parsley leaves
1 pound (455 g) fresh tomatoes, cored, diced, and frozen
Salt and freshly ground black pepper to taste
4 herb sprigs for garnish (optional)

■ Combine tomato juice, sunflower seeds, whey protein powder, lemon juice, basil, oregano, and parsley in a blender or smoothie maker. Blend on high speed for 45 seconds or until mixture is puréed and smooth. Add tomatoes, and blend on high speed again until mixture is smooth. Season to taste with salt and pepper. Serve immediately, garnished with herb sprigs, if desired.

■ **YIELD:** Four 1-cup (235-ml) servings

LYCOPENE LUSTER
TOMATO CARROT SMOOTHIE

LYCOPENE LUSTER
TOMATO CARROT SMOOTHIE

Lycopene, a phytonutrient found in tomatoes, is a powerful anti-oxidant; you can recognize it in tomatoes' deep red color. When joined with equally sweet carrots and seasoned with savory flavors including healthful garlic, this smoothie is a refreshing treat.

½ cup (120 ml) chilled carrot juice
½ cup (120 ml) chilled tomato juice
1 small carrot, scrubbed and sliced
2 scallions, trimmed and sliced
3 tablespoons (12 g) fresh cilantro leaves
2 tablespoons (28 ml) rice vinegar
2 tablespoons (30 ml) flaxseed oil
1 tablespoon (15 ml) reduced-sodium soy sauce
1 garlic clove, peeled
1¼ cups (225 g) diced tomatoes, frozen
Freshly ground black pepper to taste
4 carrot sticks or cilantro sprigs for garnish (optional)

■ Combine carrot juice, tomato juice, carrot, scallions, cilantro leaves, rice vinegar, flaxseed oil, soy sauce, and garlic in a blender or smoothie maker. Blend on high speed for 45 seconds or until mixture is puréed and smooth. Add tomatoes, and blend on high speed again until mixture is smooth. Season to taste with pepper, and serve immediately, garnished with carrot sticks, if desired.

■ **YIELD:** Four 1-cup (235-ml) servings